HIDE & SEEK

HIDE & SEEK

SUSAN GLICKMAN

SIGNAL EDITIONS IS AN IMPRINT OF VEHICULE PRESS MONTREAL CANADA

Many thanks to the Canada Council, the Ontario Arts Council, Revelina Inong, Amparo Guardiola, and Josie Cabading, for giving me the time to write this book; and to Rhea Tregebov, Carolyn Smart and Roo Borson for help along the way. Special thanks to Don Coles, for editing.

"The Lost Child: 1" was published in *Canadian Literature*; with "The Lost Child: 2" it appeared in *Prairie Schooner*. "Hide & Seek" was published in *Matrix*, and "Hunger" was a runner-up in *The Fiddlehead's* "Food for Thought" competition. Two sonnets from the "Summertime" sequence— 'Fish are Jumping ...' and 'You're gonna spread your wings ...'—appeared in *The Malahat Review*.

The quotation in "Running in Prospect Cemetery" by Rainer Maria Rilke, is from a letter to Lotte Hepner, November 8, 1915 (translated by Stephen Mitchell).

Published with the assistance of the Canada Council.

Signal Poetry series editor: Michael Harris
Edited for the press by Don Coles.
Cover art and design: J. W. Stewart
Photograph of the author: Toan Klein
Typeset by Simon Garamond.
Printed by Imprimerie d'Édition Marquis Ltée.

CANADIAN CATALOGUING IN PUBLICATION DATA

Glickman, Susan, 1953-

    Hide and seek

(Signal edition)
Poems.
ISBN 1-55065-066-1

I. Title. II. Series
PS8563.L49H53 1995   C811'.54   C95-900750-4
PR9199.3.G582H53 1995

Véhicule Press, P.O.B. 125, Place du Parc Station, Montréal, Québec H2W 2M9. Distributed in Canada and the United States by General Distribution Services, 30 Lesmill Road, Don Mills, Ontario M3B 2T6 and 4600 Witmer Industrial Estates #4, Niagara Falls, NY 14305

Printed in Canada on acid-free paper

for Jesse

"You should understand that I use my body now for everything whereas formerly I kept it away from higher regions."

—Gerald Stern, "At Bickford's"

CONTENTS

RUNNING IN PROSPECT CEMETERY

BRONWEN WALLACE
1945-1989

"—when a tree blossoms, death as well as life blossoms in it, and the
field is full of death, which from its reclining face sends forth a rich
expression of life, and the animals move patiently from one to the
other—and everywhere around us, death is at home, and it watches us
out of the cracks in Things, and a rusty nail that sticks out of a plank
somewhere, does nothing day and night except rejoice over death."

—Rainer Maria Rilke

Waiting at a bus-stop on an ordinary workday,
selecting green peppers at the market,
I am overcome by the sheer arbitrariness of my existence
in such a place at such a time
with all those others who, for the moment, preoccupied,
don't even wonder why they are here, they
and their arbitrary children succeeding their arbitrary ancestors
such random atoms organized into galaxies
of brown eyes or blue...

And then I notice my neighbour in her too-heavy coat
and praise her chapped hands weighing tomatoes
praise also her tomatoes, any tomatoes, that there should *be*
tomatoes
and she turns away from the absurd light
shining in my eyes, knowing something
is wrong, something her presence, however reassuring,
cannot remedy.
And she pays for her groceries and goes home, suddenly hungry,
and I stand over the tomatoes
the machinery of praise rusting
in my tears.

*

     Can they hear us?
     Would they want to?

I keep to the asphalt paths, heel-toe, heel-toeing it around
the perimeter of Prospect Cemetery. Late spring, early summer;
the trees flicker, the trees are licked
by yellow flame
the trees flare wholly alight now, they are
delighted altogether with being
and I with them

     but the dead, can they hear us?

*

This is a poem for my friend who always listened.
I don't know if she can hear me now
but this is a poem for her as she was then
before she went
to wherever she went to

and I "missing" her as though I had arrived a little too late,
thinking as usual there was plenty of time
and she'd just left, a hand waving goodbye from a window,
the bus gone down the lane
in a cloud of dust

and her sitting there being herself still
reading a book or talking
about to arrive somewhere else in her familiar body
tall strong & good-humoured
just *missed*
not *gone*

*

There are 26 bones in the human foot, its articulation
another form of speech. So in this running I do
I find myself conversing with those I hold
in my heart.

Therefore surely it's no insult to the dead to run
in their domain? (Although sometimes I imagine them as
elderly downstairs neighbours
grumbling about the pounding of my heels, pounding back
with spectral broomsticks
on their ceiling of roots and dirt)

And in this running I honour also
the body, which runs while it can, if it can,
to master the gestural language of bone, the syntax
of sinew. A discipline
and a celebration.

*

Body, fragile body, what
do I expect from you? Warding off with vague
prayers, promises, donations to burn units,
talking books for the blind my fear
of your vulnerability when instead I should *praise*
that you come through
as (mostly) you do. I do
except when, as now, the split between who
I think I am and what my body tells me
is too great; when in spite of my best efforts to be whole
and wholly accepting of what I am
this small frame of muscle and bone betrays
my best efforts
to be.

*

And I still want to say "you" to <u>you</u>, friend, I still want
        to talk. The space your body no longer inhabits
is an unending silence in our conversation
        and because speech for such as us is action
there are events that will never take place
        in this lifetime
without you.

And because for such as us action is speech,
        that the cancer took your mouth is both obscene
& apt. Not that you spoke ill
        but that your courage was needed
more than ever
        to speak at all.

*

Not a day this summer that I didn't think of you
and of our strange symmetry:
the cancer growing in you, the longed-for child
refusing to grow in me.
Failures of our bodies we couldn't help
but take personally, as failures
of our souls. As though we could *will* health—
as though every breath were a spiritual discipline
and our tears also, and therefore,
were another failure.

Oh my friend, sometimes I thought
I ought to be the one dying, being already
barren ground
while you are leaving your son too soon.
Not that I'd ever say anything like that to you
whose rejection of injustice was absolute, not
provisional.

But where does such injustice come from?
Even as the ground gives way beneath our feet we demand
an explanation! You missed the earthquake
in San Francisco, but let me tell you
it was a revelation to see seismologists interviewed
after the event and to realize that all they could do
was quote numbers on an arbitrary scale—like Shakespeare's star
whose worth's unknown, although his height be taken
the phenomenon remained unpredictable
and therefore unknowable.

For to know something after the fact is common sense,
not understanding. We "know" you had cancer
but not how you got it or how to treat it.
Which was why we wouldn't admit to what you had:
because to pronounce the name seemed capitulation,
belatedness, knowing something after the fact;
epitaph.

*

> *So have I seen a Flower ynn Somer Tyme*
> *Trodde down and Broke and widder ynn ytts pryme*

but here I am careful, full of care
as I am
not to tread on blossoms people leave in lieu
of words

The epigraph is from Thomas Chatterton

another language, these petals,
light as fingertips
so directly do they declare
the body's longing.

Only along the north path, no flowers;
grass overgrows the faint names
inscribed on old tombstones, paving stones
to somewhere I do not wish

to go quite yet, beyond the perfume
of tribute.
It calms me, this forgotten plot,
grief overgrown in the generations since

>   *Thomas Clark, 1865-1910*
>   *Gone to his rest in the Lord.*

When no one is looking I brush away dirt, comb back
mats of grass to divine
these fortunes. A stranger, but no less to them
than to the living

and no more, their prospect
being equally mine.

*

NOUNS unproductiveness, unproductivity, ineffectualness;
unfruitfulness, barrenness, dryness, aridity, dearth, famine;
sterileness, sterility, unfertileness, infertility, infecundity; wasted
or withered loins, dry womb; birth control, contraception,
family planning, planned parenthood; impotence.

You took the popular temperature by reading *The National
Enquirer*; suspicious of ephemera, I browse through

Roget's Thesaurus to find
more durable myths.

Here, for example,
my condition is described as both a natural disaster
like famine and as "planned parenthood"—
both definitions culminating, of course, in "impotence"

as though inability to conceive a child
precludes making love. In *Roget* as on the streets
the goal of each caress
must be a cradle.

After all, this was the summer jilted boyfriends
got injunctions against abortions, the summer
a confessed abuser demanded
a child of the woman he'd beaten,

the sterile summer I marched
for reproductive rights, the rights
of others
to have only those children they want

to have the choice I myself do not have, an irony
you would have appreciated, you,
connoisseur
of the absurd.

*

There are many theories of cancer: cancer
is a runaway virus, a cell gone mad;
cancer is an essential part of the evolutionary process,
how new variations in nature appear through cellular
modification; cancer is an overefficient parasite which,
in seeking to survive, kills its host

And humanity being an overefficient parasite which
in seeking to survive is killing the planet,
some would argue that infertility
is part of the evolutionary process,
a normal corrective whereby the expendable individual
is sacrificed for the good of the species

I myself prefer the impersonality of this scientific view
which sees us as pure potential, serene and ghostlike,
(our significance all innate, not half-accomplished)
to the more typical prejudice that we—that all victims—
must somehow deserve our illness
being weak

and therefore *worthy* of suffering
as of course from the refuge of health our critics
are not, and never will be, being able to withstand
bad genes, bad luck, war and nuclear disaster
by the force of their exceptional
will

*

Through yellow-green to green to yellow the leaves
have run their course these months I've run
beneath them. A harvest moon rises gold
as chrysanthemums over Prospect Cemetery
where sad families leave behind
their last autumn flowers.

All Souls Day and I abandon
my run, overcome by crowds whose particular griefs
I cannot share

though I have thought of their dead,
and often. Children commemorated as little lambs
and mothers as winged angels; the sober architecture
of patriarchs, all urns and columns

as though over time we grew away from nature
becoming monuments to religion or history—
as though the years took us out of and not into
our bodies.

*

ADJS unproductive, nonproductive or nonproducing; infertile,
unfertile or non-fertile; unfruitful, sterile, impotent, gelded,
acarpous, infecund, unprolific or nonprolific, ineffectual;
barren, desert, arid, gaunt, dry, dried-up, exhausted, drained,
leached, sucked dry, wasted, waste, desolate, jejune;
childless, issueless, fruitless, teemless, without issue, *sine
prole* [L]; fallow, unplowed, unsown, untilled, uncultivated;
celibate, virgin, menopausal.

*A garden inclosed is my sister, my spouse; a spring shut up,
a fountain sealed*
sang Solomon in praise of Sheba
because she was beautiful, and his, and his love was *strong
as death.*

And she sang back that *their bed was green,*
and that *as the lily among thorns,* so was her love
among the daughters. Promising
fruitfulness, for *lo, the winter was past,
the rain was over and gone*

and *the flowers appeared on the earth.*
At the same time, of course, *the fig tree put forth
her green figs*; in love's pastoral,
spring leads directly to autumn
as maiden becomes mother

in one night. In one night
bursts into bloom and then, alas, is exhausted
leached
                    dried up
                                        desolate
barren.

*

Because I never said "goodbye" our conversation's unfinished
and this shames me, that I should have been
such a coward, *unpregnant of my cause* and saying
nothing. Yes I know
the old routine—that we don't
acknowledge dying till we're forced to
so as not to give up hope—but
it's good, too, to cry together, to give up
not hope but pretence.

Because I'm not allowed to give up hope either
for myself, for my husband, for each month
our child evades us again and mourning must be resisted
again because
no one's actually died
and the pretence continues, continues, that this is
not terminal.

But infertility is another kind of death.
I remember as a child the thrill
of recognition when I understood that sometimes
doing *nothing* could be bad, that negligence
could be a crime. That's what this is,
this death of possibilities
we ignore
because it doesn't fit the known contours of grief
to mourn for one not born.
But in this, too, it resembles my missing of you

not only for who you were
but for the years I looked forward to
together, years I took for granted
to know you better in.

*

And hope is a drug, isn't it? The only one
you agreed to take after radiation failed
and the thing that had been small grew bigger, defiant
or simply oblivious, under the cover of your poor
burnt face.

At first, anyhow, the treatment hurt worse than the disease
but the doctors assured you your suffering
was worth it, as they always do, compulsive gamblers
that they are, risking nothing but a challenge
to their career average. Or, for the compassionate ones,

the human pain they try to rise above, of helplessness;
for which they console themselves by declaring
that if only you'd come to them earlier
they might have cured you. So that any error is always
the patient's, so that their magic transcends

our misery, so that they are responsible only
for success and never for failure.
Leaving us with such bewildered shame
we must do penance at their shrine, praying
that the deity who punished us with illness

will now cleanse our sinning bodies
through the ministration of these sainted healers, these
deluded Lancelots, armoured in statistics,
charging across our skins with their scalpels in pursuit of
Death who always evades them

possessing our bodies as no lover or doctor
ever can. So that this seduction by hope simply defers the day when we all,
all lovers and doctors,
collapse gratefully in those arms
extended to us, patiently, since our birth.

*

A brief thaw teases things to flower
dangerously out of season.
What are the odds on any bulb
surviving? Last year
squirrels ate my crocuses long before spring, long before the
least green antenna probed, tentatively,
sweet air.

You suggested pinks and thyme to border the rockery
but my pinks didn't make it, and last May's monster slugs
bedevilled every herb, the whole garden
their aromatic salad
before we drowned them in plates full of beer.

But I like to feed the birds, and spared
a scraggly anonymous shrub for its berries
robins love; will plant
sunflowers this summer, hollyhocks, lilac
and juniper
for juncos and cardinals to share.

If they take. The little spruce we dug up
in Quebec never put down roots
in this province, and we lost the dogwood
and the Rose of Sharon, flower
of Solomon and Sheba. In Prospect Cemetery

the Rose of Sharon flourishes
as all trees do; among the conifers flaunts
her sensual purple.
Rooted, those blooms revive each season
where other flowers fail,
cut down, strewn on tombstones

whose elegies they reprise
in their fading.

*

running cold running quick the breath
a fog through which, avidly, winter bites

the closest I'll ever come to breathing
underwater——

breathing something solid
instead of this too easily invisible air

known only now
as ice

known, as all things are,
by definition, in opposition

present most
as absence

Oh, in my day-to-dailiness I do not praise
the absent or unspoken more

than that which is declared openly
however brokenly

but this is for my friend who is dead
this is for my child who is not born

this is a poem that should be all
white space

THE LOST CHILD

We thought you were just down in the garden
playing, we thought you could hear us, we thought
as soon as we called
you'd come home.
So when I asked your father to get you he said
"Let's wait a little longer"—after all,
wasn't it yesterday we too had been children?
And when he felt it was time I
wasn't quite ready.
Everything had to be perfect: the furniture polished,
linen ironed, your birthday candles lit.
Then we called and called

through the appleblossom, the mist, the warm spring rain;
through the long summer's grasses, the slanting light the dancing
maddened flies; through the bruised leaves of one fall
and another; the drifts
of one desolate winter, and another
but you didn't hear us you didn't come—
where had you wandered to, Darling, where?

How helpless we were, how foolish we felt
before the detectives, their fancy machines
and tracker dogs. We answered their questions
and endured their inspection
and searched with them again and again all
your hiding places, looking
for a footprint, a strand of hair, a forgotten
toy. Anything, anything

to show you *had* been there, you *might* return
and then suddenly after all there you were, quite calm
and happy, waiting for us, in your own patch of sunlight
in your own private meadow, no sun warmer
no flower sweeter
than you. Oh
you were never lost, dear child, you were
just not yet found.

"as if spirit attended to plainness only, the more complicated forms
exhausting it"

> —Robert Hass, "Spring Drawing"

1.Sundays in the Park

Having waited as long as anyone might who thought the world conformable
to desire, they were dumbstruck to discover it was not. Not that they *had*
any such convictions but innocence, after all, may be nothing more than
the absence of a sense of mortality. And by this measure she had been
more innocent than most—for until now she had experienced life as pure
happenstance. So she had to learn, terribly and at once, the heft and music
of all that might have been.

She keeps slipping irresistibly from the collective to the singular, as they
both were to do in the childless months & years that followed. As we all
do, being unable to experience tragedy as communal except on public
occasions. Each alone in the same bed they dreamed the same dream: a
small trusting form holding their hand under an avenue of bright leaves.
What persists is this vision, the phantom feel of little fingers.

2. Mission Control

What persists is the body's conviction, held tight in each coil of DNA, that it can achieve its mission. Deaf to the head's chatter about social responsibility & the environment, the heart's terror of poison & knives, the cells hum lullabies to each other.

Sweet sweet sweetly they sing lyrics we knew before we knew our own names. And now the future becomes familiar: imageless speculation transformed into everything best known and best loved in the past. Our genes, ever sentimental, abhor singularity.

3. Row Row Row Your Boat

Science can only take you so far but as far as science could go, they went. Tests and more tests, surgery and more surgery. None as painful as the glib advice of those safely on shore: "Just relax, you're trying too hard." Those who still believed, as they once did, in free will.

Are there ever any new stories, even in this brave new world? "Providence," she said (who would disclaim trust in anything more than existential roulette—if asked). Now more than ever she understood that most things were beyond her control. This was both humiliating and wonderful. To float, directionless as her little passenger. Just to float.

4. Hide & Seek

But what of that other voyager, in his sleep of pure dream? A darkness dimly red; a cave of echoes; the sweetest sea. Who can know what he knew then or remembered later? The language of that country has never been translated.

But beyond language they began to know each other—he their voices, they his touch. Hearing them sing, he calmed; feeling him kick, they laughed; hearing them laugh, he kicked again. A nine months' game of hide & seek. Wondering, sometimes, who would emerge from the scary closet, the spider-webbed space under the stairs.

5. So Big!

Bigger than a breadbox, certainly; sometimes she feels bigger than a volkswagon. How can so tiny a creature demand so much space? So much fuel? So much breath? But their body—for it was no longer accurate to speak of it as hers—embraced this new role as fervently as an understudy finally called to the stage. All those years of suspicion & mistrust: she wishes she could take them back.

And yet, even now, this body imposed on her, made a pose of her. No woman could ever simply be, it seemed; it seemed that her abundance was metaphor, her belly and breasts metonymy, for something always bigger than herself.

6. Lady Madonna

Free at last from all self-consciousness, she parades the streets. Traffic parts like the waters before the Queen Mary. Strangers wave banners, enthusiastically, from shore. What did she do to deserve this universal applause? And does it actually have anything to do with *her*?

Yes & No. No, & again Yes. She has been transformed into a mythic creature before whom even her own knees bend. The gravity of the oath she has sworn burns brightly in her spine. More public than the marriage vow, it too joins more than two people. More intimate than conjugal passion is this love that makes her weep mornings over the newspaper/ nights in front of the TV. Mothers and children. Mothers and children. This love that joins her to others also joins them to her.

7. Rock-a-bye Baby

Dreams of missed buses, trains, airplanes; lost luggage, stolen documents. Dreams of murderous strangers; dreams of adulterous liasons. Dreams of home renovation. Dreams of food—many many dreams of food. Dreams of dreams within dreams all those narcotic afternoons, sinking willy-nilly into the arms of Morpheus

(as, months of midnights later, she'd rouse to find the baby finally asleep at her breast, herself asleep in the rocker, each lulled by the other's presence into sweet somnolence. At which time there would no longer be any dreams at all)

8. Happy Birthday

Birth is what he does; to describe what she does as "labour" is an understatement. Except that even now she feels strangely disconnected from the hard & beautiful work of her body, performing as it does like a trained gymnast—though she doesn't remember ever doing any training. How tedious all those years of running & swimming & skiing must have been to a secret group of muscles which vaunt their extraordinary abilities as she observes, astonished, from the sidelines.

As she will continue to observe in the endless days that follow (delirious from lack of sleep, loony from lack of fellowship) the automatic mothering gestures enacted by her arms, the appropriate murmurs from her lips. *Who is doing all this, and where did she learn it? And when will I wake up?*

CALM SEA, PROSPEROUS VOYAGE

After waiting so many years
what's a few more days?

Days that pass in a haze of last-minute shopping
for tiny socks and hats
(so tiny they require the utmost scrutiny
just to be seen)

as those last minutes expand with the universe
within which I too expand

orbiting the summer streets of this city
with you at my centre

...

You are so quiet, comparatively, lodged tight in your nest.
Our conversation of knees and elbows is muted now, though I still
chat to you in the bath. Singing "Where's my baby?" till you
reply, a small bump on the enormous hill of (what was) my belly.
I have never been so happy as during these nine months.

...

Every baby I see makes me cry.
Why is this? Your father asks.
If he doesn't know, I can't tell him.

...

Baby baby, I need you
Oooh Baby Baby, Baby I love you
I got you, Babe
Be my, be my little baby

Wouldn't you agree that, Baby, you and me
have got a groovy kind of love?

...

Two days of such pain
I almost forget why I'm here
think I'll just go home now
and read a good book

Just kid-ding.

Let's practise breathing
as if our lives depended on it

...

My arms anticipate you, my arms already
know your shape, my mouth
the sweet nape of your neck, black silk
of your hair, little fists curled like ferns
beside the flower of your face

When finally *finally* you are born you could be no other child
we fit together again as fast as we can
don't ask me to let you go
too soon

HUNGER

"Is man then meant to spurn the gifts of Nature? Has he been born but to pluck the bitterest fruits? For whom do those flowers grow, that the gods make flourish at mere mortals' feet?...It is a way of pleasing Providence to give ourselves up to the various delights which she suggests to us; our very needs spring from her laws, and our desires from her inspirations."

—Epicurus

(money to burn)

so there we were in Mexico again
trying to decide what would be a "good buy"
from the young basketmaker
waiting patiently under a tree in Oaxaca all day
for tourists to leave their fancy hotels
with money to burn

us with more cash in our pockets than she earns in a year
and still haggling because
it's the custom
(and also to rationalize our greed)

and she waiting with such solicitude
expecting us to haggle

so that I got sick; my body
purging itself because I had consumed
too much
bleeding as though in apology for having
(I'm sorry) too much

in Chiapas with my three pairs of shoes
where the Chomulan women go barefoot after marriage
in sign of subservience to their husbands

flat brown feet, dirty leather
plodding in from the villages
with one real baby and a sack full of dolls
to sleep overnight in the rain in the zocalo
waiting for tourists

without shame

following the tourists without shame into and out of
hotels, restaurants; insistent fistsful of
red or blue woolen dolls or shawls
needing money to burn firewood
this cold winter

The "zocalo" is a public square

(cold winter)

a "biting" wind, we say; we say we live
in its teeth
at the mouth of the river, in the eye
of the storm

as though the body of the world consumed us
as we consume it

(consume it)

so that entering the sweater department of any fancy store I am *stricken*
with (what seems) a visceral need to have, I need to have them all, all the
colours, the soft brightness, as though a rainbow of wool were our best
insurance against any future sorrow; so that I am absurdly tearful among
the cashmeres and mohairs, the lambswools and silk-and-polyester blends,
grieving for all lost, for all elusive beauty

or alternatively, cruising the buffet table at a cousin's expensive wedding,
I feel glutted before venturing one bite: the impossibility of tasting
everything makes tasting *anything* redundant, a feast of Tantalus however
much I eat; the poached salmon and caesar salad, the chocolate mints, the
so festive and dainty cakes which will have vanished by the time I am hungry
again

(hungry again)

that I have been, always, ashamed of this hunger
confusing it with greed
as though simply to *acknowledge* simple appetite
were suspect

as though my body had no rights

so that I spent most of my life wishing away
(fasting away, running away)
hips, thighs, breasts
and the dreaded belly

trying to expiate the guilt of being a consumer
with exercise and fasting
ignoring what the language tells us:

that when we are lonely
we feel hollow and empty;
that we fear lean years, a slim purse,
insubstantial rumours, scant causes,
narrow minds

(narrow minds)

minds narrow as the waists we wish for women
(we women wish for)

Victorian ladies never ate in public lest such a display suggest unmaidenly desire. Being modern, we think it sexy to appear asexual; "lean and mean" as teenage boys. All eyes and hair, like little girls. Vampiric lips, to remind us that women's hunger is deadly.

while the language teaches
to be satisfied one must have enough
to be content, have contents
be in clover

      feel one's oats

               be full of beans

the origin of all such talk
the blunt and truthful belly

belly that ties itself in knots, clenches or heaves,
speaking thus, sometimes, against what we think we know
about who we think we are

belly that betrays
our betrayals of the belly

(of the belly)

and of the legs, buttocks, breasts
of all soft skin and supple muscle
of all sweet motion and salt desire
I sing

our birthright
the twoness that is one
so close
you cannot distinguish where skin meets skin
whose breath/ whose heart

is it discretion or dismay, that keeps secret
this joyful solace? that we are all
still children

redeems the body's desires, this is
necessary as air this is not
gluttony
but survival

(survival)

that this needs no translation
this most authentic hunger
for which milk is metaphor

is why no one speaks of it, it being
immeasurable
and lost

a void we avoid by buying
things
becoming consumers

consumed with loneliness for
the twoness that is one

douceur de vivre it is
we have forgotten, been made
to forget

because it is not profitable
to acknowledge our nature
as nature

no goods can come of it

O shame of naked breast and greedy infant mouth!
O shame of flesh-surrender, acknowledging we are
all food!

(all food)

the riddle the sphinx would have asked Jocasta
had it been she at the crossroads:

> who is both eater
> and that which is eaten
> ?

the answer = one who has a bun in the oven

(that we say "the baby is in mommy's tummy"
has as much to do with reason as with rhyme)

> "I could just eat him up!"
> grandma nibbles
> babysoft neck and toes

(toes)

which the baby too loves better
than any toy, unloseable pink digits wriggling
at the end of his gaze

his glee at discovering they belong to him
more loveable if less dextrous
than fingers

more loveable because
for *he-who-cannot-walk-yet*
their function is pure delight

(pure delight)

no delight so pure as an infant's
uncompelled joy in being

here, now, this
creaturely congress
of feelings

tactile & emotional
both, both
bewildering

that he takes in
with his mother's familiar milk

that he gives out
with each lovely insistent cry

(cry)

INSTRUCTIONS:

1. Sterilize bottles, nipples, caps and utensils by boiling 5 minutes in a large pot
or sterilizer.
2. Clean top of can and pour boiling water over it.
3. Shake can very well and open with pull-ring.
4. Pour formula into bottles and put on nipples and caps taking care not to touch
tops of nipples.
5. Warm to room or body temperature before feeding. Discard unused formula
after feeding.
6. Prepared formula should be stored in a refrigerator and used within 24-48
hours. Keep unused formula in covered can under refrigeration and use within
24-48 hours after opening.

INGREDIENTS:

water, whey powder (demineralized), coconut oil, skim milk powder, soybean oil, lactose, mono and diglycerides, potassium citrate, calcium chloride, soybean lecithin, carrageenan, sodium ascorbate, sodium citrate, taurine, di-alpha tocosulfate, calcium pantothenate, cupric sulfate, vitamin a palmitate, thiamine hydrochloride, pyridoxine, hydrochloride, cholecalciferol, manganese sulfate, folic acid, vitamin k, biotin and vitamin b12.

O shame of naked breast
and greedy infant mouth

shame

(shame)

because it is not profitable to acknowledge our nature
as nature
no goods can come of it

because infancy has no schedule
and appetite refutes logic

because pregnancy is the greatest privilege
and also the greatest indignity

because only women get pregnant
because only women have breasts

because I could get drunk on the smell of babies' skin
because skin is rebel territory
and babies are all subversives

because women's bodies change monthly
in defiance of social order

because formula costs money
and breastmilk is free

because a nursing baby makes greedy sucking noises
in defiance of social order

because he pats your breast and strokes your face
and this is the purest possession

because it feels good
and no goods can come of it

because it feels so good

(so good)

Oh little one
imagine the world and have it come
at your least whimper

(I do)

THE LOST CHILD

She wandered away and no one noticed, but now
she's returned—
a little hesitant, perhaps, for those
lost years; a little clumsy
at play

Send her to the garden to pull weeds
Let her not worry about which are weeds and which
respectable flowers

Let her jump in the mud with yellow rubber boots
let her jump in the mud barefoot

let her swing in the hammock and not consult
her watch
let her frolic with the baby
according to his measure

let the baby pull her hair and shout *Boo*
and let her pretend to be terrified

let the baby be delighted
let them be monsters all afternoon

and all night too if they wish

let them lurk behind sofas and under
kitchen tables
let them interrogate the grain of the floorboards
and make funny faces in the reflecting oven-door

let their house be a museum of laughter

let new alphabets flood the bathroom
while tentacles creep from the tub
to seize a toothbrush

let everyone brush their teeth in time to this music
let them sing the same lullabies every night
and rejoice in the repetition

let everything familiar enchant them
let everything unfamiliar enchant them

let the baby explore her face casually
with his fingers and mouth
let her be home to him
let her be home

SUMMERTIME

Summertime, and the living is easy

Coming between us to bring us together
little bean. Your role; as mine was to go
trippingly, maternal bulk aglow—
warm with sweet thoughts of becoming your mother.
So comfortable-hazy then I thought I knew
what a pleasure it would be: summer
all year long; long days of lengthening wonder
and serious play. No tropical storms blew
in my fantasy! But sleeplessness day
after weary day left our tempers raw,
hearts subdued by responsibility.
"Family" displaced "romance", as others foresaw.
(Novices, we made the trade willingly—
what greater joy than being *Dada, Mama?*)

Fish are jumping, and the cotton is high

At first the slightest ripple, unfamiliar
as all sensations are below the chin
in this body I stubbornly call "mine"
then something fiercer; newer; was it your
knee or elbow WHOOPS there it goes again I
never experienced anything so odd—
this must be what it feels like to be God
with all creation rattling round your belly!
I like your Aunt Lisa's description best:
a goldfish nosing up against the glass.
Blind appetite? Affection? Wanderlust?
Perhaps all three. I know; I too have wished
to be both in and out; to get some rest
and yet to have you always here like this.

And "the earth is all before you where to choose."
Fat chance! But without such illusions
who'd sacrifice a baby to pollution,
lies and violence; the tightening global noose?
Not us. For ages we used these fears
to put off more personal confrontations
till nature hit us with the revelation
of what was passing us by with the passing years.
So, yes, I'm grateful, dazed by the miracle
I'm not sure I deserve, but wondering
if what we've done is very selfish still.
Do you *want* to be here, little wrinkled thing,
cold and sleepless; lonely; never full?
All we can do is hold you now, and sing.

So hush, little baby, don't you cry

In fact, you wailed before you were fully born.
Appalled by hospital noise, electric light
and chilly air? Or maybe it wasn't fright
but eagerness: blowing your own horn?
We'd like to think so, though you cried a lot
for someone simply announcing his arrival—
six weeks worth; the record is archival
if hastily scrawled, tear-smeared, poorly blotted.
Your baby book's the only thing I wrote
those early months, too bewildered, almost,
to talk. The occasional thank-you note
depleted what little fluency I'd boast
I had; had had; would have again—I hoped.
For now we clung to each other: both lost.

One of these mornings, you're gonna rise up singing

At nine months old, you conduct opera
to the radio; point to the CD player
when you want to dance. We say we don't care
what you do when you grow up, etcetera,
but seize each bogus clue with true conviction—
your very diapers oracular. Forgive us.
Your Mom and Dad are daft, inanely curious
about who you are, will be; a prediction
anyone could have made, and did, but we
thumbed our noses at a year ago.
Like everyone who's ever had a baby
we find our best intentions hard to follow;
to do right by you is not so easy
(which we thought we knew—but then, how could we know?).

It kind of caught us sideways, your first word:
in the midst of undistinguished babble
and humming (mouth full) at the kitchen table
you pointed out the window and said "bird!"
Then for three weeks your vocabulary
flourished daily—"up" & "down" & "apple"
"Daddy" & "Mama," "octopus" & "ball"—
until those first steps, tentative and wary.
I'm like that too, I have to concentrate
on one thing at a time; in this case, you.
Which is why I've done so little work of late
or exercise, or anything you can't do
with me or on me. You'll have to liberate
us from each other before the year is through.

But till that morning, ain't no one gonna harm you

The little boy's hand, his hand full of trust,
trustingly offered to the bigger boy
as, without looking back, he walked away
from his mother to be beaten to death. Almost
more than I could bear, seeing in that slight back
turned forever, leaving forever, yours
as you walk off innocently towards
some horror I will fail to expect
or, worse, anticipate but not forestall.
Whenever I'm not holding you I know
nothing's *childproof*: no house, school, shopping mall,
no car, no bicycle. Nowhere to go
on God's green earth where children cannot fall
from mothers' arms. No. Nowhere to go.

With Mommy and Daddy standing by

Next week's your *Happy Birthday*, monkey boy.
Uncanny how these past twelve months have flown!
Back then I thought I'd never last till noon
nursing you, changing you, every hour or two;
today you prefer to take milk from a cup
and try to join our dinner conversation,
or disrupt it with perpetual motion.
From your perch you screech "Go down," then holler "UP!"
fervently ambivalent. Desire
is what you're all about. Even Mother
is no longer just a fact of nature—
you *choose* me; other times you choose your father.
Last year we were entranced. But this summer
we'll become a family truly, and together.

Our son was due in June, so we lullabied him prenatally with the Gershwin ballad, "Summertime." When he took his first breath and started to cry, his father began to sing the song to him. He instantly hushed. "Summertime" remained his special song for a long time.

POEMS NO ONE WRITES

for Jesse at two

Who is he, this diminutive male person
vrooooming around the living room? One minute he is
all self-possession: "I'm BIG;
I can use the lawnmower." The next,
he whimpers at my knee "Cuddle me, cuddle me,
Mama."

Why does he love trucks & baseball? Why
kick his vanilla-scented baby doll
with the realistically opening-and-shutting blue eyes
across the room and down the stairs?
Who taught him to be a cartoon boy?

The mothers in the park confer. Hormones
are a topic of endless diversion here. We know
exactly how irresistible they are, having been
beaten to our knees bearing these same cherubs who now
dig & swing & slide together
in their brief commonwealth.
Other people's children also smell sweet
around the neck and shoulders. It's June
and sunscreen masks them a little, and the odours of hot cotton,
sand, and apple juice, but they're still unmistakably
small mammals, and ours.

Poems no one writes occupy our days. We hitchhike
their imaginations; it takes all morning to walk one block
there being so many creatures and crevices and bicycles
and mailboxes to examine along the way.
Love is in the details, someone said.
I don't know who—that's the kind of thing
I don't know anymore. But it's true.
The infant whose suckling once healed my womb
now cries out in his sleep when I dream he has fallen;

looks up from play to tell me what I am thinking.
And when I ask if he saw a picture in my head,
he says "Yes" quite simply
and returns to his game.

---

line 4: read as "yawnmower"

SIGNAL EDITIONS

BEDROCK David Solway
THE SIGNAL ANTHOLOGY Edited by Michael Harris
MURMUR OF THE STARS: SELECTED SHORTER POEMS
        Peter Dale Scott
WHAT DANTE DID WITH LOSS Jan Conn
MORNING WATCH John Reibetanz
JOY IS NOT MY PROFESSION Muhammad al-Maghut
        Translated by John Asfour and Alison Burch
WRESTLING WITH ANGELS: SELECTED POEMS Doug Beardsley
HIDE & SEEK Susan Glickman
MAPPING THE CHAOS Rhea Tregebov
FIRE NEVER SLEEPS Carla Hartsfield

SIGNAL
EDITIONS

PRINTED BY
IMPRIMERIE D'ÉDITION MARQUIS
IN AUGUST 1995
MONTMAGNY (QUÉBEC)